CW01263181

Gallery Books
Editor Peter Fallon
NATIONAL THEATRE

John McAuliffe

NATIONAL THEATRE

Gallery Books

National Theatre
is first published
simultaneously in paperback
and in a clothbound edition
on 10 October 2024.

The Gallery Press
Loughcrew
Oldcastle
County Meath
Ireland

www.gallerypress.com

*All rights reserved. For permission
to reprint or broadcast these poems,
write to The Gallery Press:*
books@gallerypress.com

© John McAuliffe 2024

The right of John McAuliffe to be identified as Author of this Work has been asserted in accordance with Section 77 of the Copyright, Designs and Patents Act 1988.

ISBN 978 1 91133 886 4 *paperback*
      978 1 91133 887 1 *clothbound*

A CIP catalogue record for this book
is available from the British Library.

National Theatre receives financial assistance
from the Arts Council of Ireland.

Contents

Fathom *page* 11
The Salt Cellar 12
National Theatre 14
Two Trees 15
My Golf Game 16
Prep 17
Flight 18
The Tears 19
One Place 20
Folk Song 22
Parlour 23
The Mountain 24
The Retainers 25
Fog Lane 28
The End of Fear 30
Testing, Testing 33
The Scientific Method 34
The Seven Hills: G20 at Trevi Fountain, 2021 35
Influencer on Lake Como 42
Bonn 43
The Border Shuts 44
The Call 46
Black Box 48
The River 49
Souterrain 50
Every Martini 52
The Herons 55
Florida 56
A Sign 57
The Fire Officer 58
The Prospect 59
Sarcococca confusa, or Sweet Box 60

Acknowledgements 62

for Róisín and Ronan and Clíona

for Nancy

Fathom

Full of joy and holiday and shouting, 'First',
I dived, forgetting until I emerged
from the freezing wave half-blind
my glasses, gone into the Irish Sea, the kids
rummaging in the sand: it flashed
before us, Day 1 of this time away,
its piles of books and new destinations,
and not seeing what was in front of me,
the tide wasting the sand
as it made for the dunes and marl-cliff,
the kelp and shells and stones —
which I'd be led around later,
more soberly, and the fuss
of their having to be pointed out and described —
when one of the kids, I couldn't see which,
rising out of the water, 'Found them'.

The Salt Cellar

after Horace Ode 2.16

1

A cloud drifts across the sea
and across the moon's reflection in the sea,
so a sailor out there loses sight of the star in the west;
so a quiet life goes out, which he suddenly wants.

The quiet life is what a man thinks about when his ruler
builds a case for war. A quiet life's what a sailor,
even as he boasts about promotion, prays for.
The places he'll go are not the life he wished for.

Who wants the ruler's lectern, its reminder that treasure
is to be fought over . . . Go home late, get up earlier:
time's anxious grip tightens when word
from a well-appointed room sends its delegates abroad.

2

Interesting times are no concern of this sailor's sister.
She will sit them out at a table decorated by a salt cellar
handed down through generations. Such is a house
whose sleep is undisturbed by stupid desires.

Why does anyone talk up glory and the touch of fame,
or a faraway second home?
As if time can be divided, and who we are, or have been,
changed by a change of scene.

Disaster's indiscriminate, pushes the latest tycoon off his
   yacht,
sidles up to a magnate's Learjet,

and overtakes the eastern gales which have yet
to return our brother to the harbour from which he sailed out.

3

No one of us is set up in a palace,
inland, in sight of the Aegean's blues,
with fields of prime Sicilian cattle and tenants
from the converted outhouses who drop by
with not just rent but presents,

wool twice-dyed in fashionable colours . . . It is
luck, instead — all of it —
to have a smallish house outside the fray,
no time to be envious,
and a feeling for whatever inspiration blows this way.

National Theatre

for Tim Price

In the film he has been adapting for the stage
we can't stop laughing at the opening scene — man, woman,
   child,
a family, sit at a table in a ski resort's conservatory
as what looks like a snow shower
develops into what looks like an avalanche
so that the husband, father, main man first says, It's nothing,
   as he starts to inch

and, taking fright, runs away, saving he presumes his skin.
And when it isn't an avalanche, but a passing snow shower,
must crawl through settling dust to what he abandoned,
and won't recover from, what looked like an avalanche
disclosing somehow that what looked like a family,
what looked, for better or worse, like a marriage, was not
   that, not exactly.

What is the avalanche but this, we are laughing still —
his folding under pressure so unfortunately applied
until he is true to himself. And my friend is wondering too
at how the theatre must devise this snowstorm, which isn't;
and I'm thinking of how what people say stirs up storms of
   hot air
a good life must navigate and sail through to actual rough
   water.

And the conversation turns, inland again, to what
on earth is happening at the Abbey, and what in god's name
is the story at NTW, and we are talking
while the enormous wave of white noise
angles our way in the wings
from where we can't even see the weak layer it finds in things.

Two Trees

1 SMOKE TREE

She walks out the front door
into the first bird-haunted morning of spring

holding what could be a pot plant in front of her.
Smoke trails up from her sheltering hand.

2 SYCAMORE

*The leaves to the sycamore return
and altered by its shadows we recline,*

just lying here as days and hours extend,
the pigeons ebbing into the light.

Daylight and the traffic's slowed pulse, a gleam
the shadows cross at intervals, a light that

(eaten into, hawthorn-blossom-dotted, fallen,
summer going) has one last splash of orange, pink

we'll remember in stars the night revolves.
Helicopters, birdsong, the end of days, and out

along the infinite lanes and tree-lined roads
is tracery, futures going cold. The year turns.

My Golf Game

A boiling day, took a hammer to the shed, broke down
    the struts,
smashed the planks off, pried away the corner nails,
cut free the tarp roof, worn through in places so it leaked
decades of weather onto rusted garden tools, firewood

and a bag of golf clubs I'd brought over in 2002.
When I stepped on the flattened wall now laid on its side,
felt the air leave the sole of my holed shoe.
Put the clubs to one side under the magnolia,

bagged and wheeled out the rest in batches, loaded the boot,
dragged the door out last, knocking a can of blue paint
which, when I emptied a gardening can, meaning to clear
    it, spread the stain.
Closed the boot, pushing the shed door so it, just, touches
    the front windscreen.

Out back, an empty space next to where the golf bag stands
    (still does)
at the edge of the bluish flags, and the upright kitchen brush
I'd used to sweep the hundreds of nails and debris
into a brown pile. Like a scale model, with turbines, of the
    Ribble Valley —

a post-industrial wasteland. I'm wedged into the pulled-
    forward seat,
crouched, peering over the driver's wheel: the wood smell,
planks lined up by my head, above me, to each side,
paint on my nose, the rear view the intact door. Well.

Prep

The magazine flops open on the kitchen table.
The window admits the pinkish light.
'Is it ready?' the eldest calls. The fridge is an option
when the recipe on *Good Food* advises using *chervil*.
The chopping board is cleaned, the knife is out.
He'll wait a minute, turn the page to the cartoon.
There's a space where there should be a caption.

The chicken's a mess he subdivides,
a slippery, uneven pile-up that seems larger,
chopped, than it did 'whole'. He decides,
imagining the youngest on 'chervil', that omission's better,
and dices an onion, teary while the news goes over
the same tune he'd left the house not quite singing
ten hours earlier with daylight coming:

Call the kids. Clear the table. Hurry up,
this shouldn't take years. A lifetime! Clean the counter.
Get the key, someone must go for milk to the shop.
Remind him about biscuits, says his sister,
following her brother. So they all round the corner.
Everything is cooking. He reads on from back to front,
head bent to a silence night has darkened.

Head bent to a silence night has darkened.
Everything is cooking. He reads on from back to front.
Following her brother, so they all round the corner,
'remind him about biscuits,' says his sister.
Get the key. Someone must go for milk to the shop.
This shouldn't take *years*. A lifetime! Clean the counter.
Call the kids. Lay the table. Hurry *up*.

Flight

I am distracted, happily explaining exam technique
for bringing in evidence — a question, a graphic —
to make a good point stick,
but also showing how it sticks, i.e., answering a specific
question but always drawing in the machinery that's been
    mastered —
anacoluthon, say, meaning a change of direction
or metaphor, bringing one thing to life with another
and, yes, I'm droning about this when I should be online,
checking departures to the new place, the price absurd,
but sailing instead of flying, doing the right thing

which, we all realize, will be after you finish: my comprehension,
suddenly, of our element changing, its coming translation
arriving when you glance up from the table for a sec:
'and now he smiled as he softened the wax
with his thumb, poking around in what his parent's hand had
    made fine,
although the whole would still hang together,
Daedalus steadying himself on the spine,
fitting his arms to the wings too, afloat so, initially, they go
    together.'

The Tears

Who doesn't know what will break,
into pieces, the city and the oak,
the ledge of the cliff and the climber's cuticle,
the shipyard breaker and the terminal,
the factory floor and the honest worker,
the union rep's loyalty to her officer,
the office-worker's home station and his cubicle,
the historian's writ and who says what was meant,
the vestiges of courts and parliament
worn down into granular details; child and parent,
the portrait painter and the carpenter,
the wooden table and formica counter,
the motorway slip road and the mastodon's skeleton,
the linear equation to the nearest decimal,
the wormy earth and the last May daffodil,
the national flag and the flag of hopeful green stuff woven,
the trembling hand on the tiller and each alternate version,
the proverbs which squat on the event horizon:
the Lord gave; a bang and whimper; the tears.
Your remembrances are as ashes.

One Place

I'd met him for years at the school gate,
tall, shambling, fair-haired, but had no name
to put to his face when I saw him on a park bench,
standing up as I approached, enjoying his own

Tuesday 'hiatus'. I asked what he did
that allowed him such afternoons. He was not the kind
who declares 'I prefer not to be defined by work',
explaining how a survey matches a contract's black and
   white

to, say, an overgrown, culverted quarter acre.
I knew the place he meant. Rights of way, ancient lights —
another term I knew, from a poem. After years in one place
he'd made contacts, was freelance, his wife

full-time, a head, the youngest gone to high school,
explaining these afternoons, and why I had not seen him
at the primary of late. He has time now, he says,
when he reviews the jobs he gets, to factor in

all sorts: how a nearby bridge brings together, in iron
and rust, a view of a river, the name of a local warden,
a golf course *and* the main road to the airport.
And he misses nothing about his old institution,

its tense recoveries, its suddenly changed relations:
there, to ask a question was to get only a reputation
for asking questions. He never gives a second thought,
he says, to missing out on the current boom,

the city looming, a metal forest,
fortunes gambled on each dead cert development . . .
Now, for houses, he says, like yours or mine, he looks longer
at things others would confess they have not seen,

even as the world is more and more like an altered
photo of itself. There are drones for my line of work,
he says, edging his foot on and off the footpath,
drawing a sort of line in the earth as he does so,

a plot under his foot that he points to,
a yellow-green example he scrubs
from the park's larger brown and green and grey,
as the gusty little and large of spring rain

reminds him — it is too late for me to ask his name —
to say goodbye, he must collect his daughter
as I must mine, so we walk into the familiar gloom,
lights coming on in the houses at the perimeter.

Folk Song

1

Women were turned to the right, men braced on their left side,
each settled on a fern cot and wrapped in hide,
high hopes buried with a dog's jaw, a bracelet, daggers
and, near the young men's pelvises, decorated beakers.
In the underworld, best to be prepared.
Someone made an effort, like a mourner
these days who looks for the right word.

2

The curlew's quick call seems to come from nowhere,
mid-air, where new life hurries out after the scent of water,
threading structures that still sound over
the blank foreheads of a walking son and daughter,
other contributions brought to light,
as the head turns. Days in the sun which don't last

or find their level in a gesture, in *I'm a free man on Sunday*
or a gait, sloping up, hoping that it is *I'll lie
where the bracken is deep* or *The heather
has oft been my bed* that will remember

my hours in the song-crossed blue, alive in the hall of the
    elements,
four winds peppered with rain, birdsong, a glance
at the places we scale, and crowds of us marching uphill
where microgliders, as they will, gravely spiral out of sight.

Parlour

A big mantelpiece.
And a crowded dresser
the woman of the house
might have stood in front of,
a *parlour*. There's the piano,
next to the window.

She swings her arms
when the musicians pile in,
then fingers are flying
along frets and keys.
A tune, or a song? The air
is easy on the ear

and their friends are
a few minutes later
putting their hands together
and asking for more,
not so much singing along
as joining in.

The Mountain

The wrong hill climbed the wrong way
brought the same view,
grey, brown, green sieving each other
and the mountain still one valley over.

The heather and furze
lie low and brighten, and we visitors,
finding no purchase, blank
on the cross-country walk
seen so clearly as local, doable,
from the back window of a harbour rental.

Now is the time to sit down
at the kitchen table, finding another form
for the mountain, its blue reflection
a closed system we descend from.

The Retainers

1

The red discarded cup is half in, half out of the frozen gully.
In it dregs harden, caught in the groundswell,
a brown eye alive in the deep freeze of the turning circle,
glazed, blind, out of the swim, a hopeless jelly

stuck in what happened around it,
no longer even reflective, only waiting
for someone to take it away.
Being seen by it is like catching a flu,
                                bothering, awful, shivering,

but to anyone not under its weather
nothing special and, even to the patient,
                                      forgotten, after.
How *become* this, something passed around and left,
nothing deliberate in its always being, somewhere,
                                that could be called a cause.
Mulled over, that eye in the slush accuses still.
All it has is an excuse.

2

The shoe is an old battered brogue, a man's shoe, one of a pair.
Out in the weather weeks the pinking in it is all that's fine.
Maybe its partner is still laced across a phone-wire,
their separation the work of unseen hands. This one,
its tongue and muck-clotted sole are equally aflap,
its eyelets widening, its shoelace a frayed grey zag
of lightning. Its rain-wet magpie shine.
It does, in spite of everything, this left shoe,
                                do more than speak for just itself.

3

The green bin on its side, with its lid gone,
tilted athwart the road and footpath
is like the one I had whose lid one day would not shut.
In it a fortnight worth of coffee grounds, stews of skin,

ligament, eggshells, the last fresh stalks and first ash,
but not so full it would not close the night before.
Turning it towards the street
I saw the rat and how it was caught

in the gap it had chewed, its claws and head
wedged through the hole,
but the body, too full of whatever it had found,
completely stuck, its claws not moving any longer, its
    eyes still.

The bin on its side was empty,
ready for collection,
with those telltale holes chewed under the rim.
I would have liked to leave or throw ours away

but righted the lid and took a spade's edge to the body,
then used a plastic bag
to pull the upper body, the head and shoulders free,
before I reached in with the bag, returned it to its other half

and, given that it was not green waste, deposited the lot,
as if such things could be tidied away,
in the other bin, out of sight
until the following week's collection day.

4

Parked on the footpath across from the hospital,
the white block of fridge, a bar fridge,
shelters weeds which root in its mossy edge
among the empties and butts and matches
it is beyond some of our wherewithal
to quit.
Amazing to see its whiteness,
storing nothing, set off such green growth.

Fog Lane

In the woods the mother goose covers her three young
    swimmers with a wing
and the fox tiptoes and braces herself at the railing.
There is a path from the road to the water I take each
    morning
letting the dog, who lately knows the difference between
    ball and bird,
off the lead to which he will return when I make a sign
    and say the word.

But a morning comes when mules, carrying the material
they are saddled with, get across and muddle the marginal
lines that join and separate the road and water and wood,
their heads close to the ground when the green parakeets
chop and scream in the middle air above the park they turn
    to dust and mud.

My neighbour, who is older, says that when she meets
the park mules dragging gravel into the green and making
    the paths mud
and draining the pool where the birds swim and the fox waits,
she remembers once seeing, near here, a low line of toads,
not frogs she insists, toads, a long mass on the move on
    main and side roads,

pilgrims from a new estate's built-over, culverted river,
squads of them noisily making their way — she doesn't
    know where.
They must have been starving, she says, the toads slowly
    moving east,
and could not even have known they were lost.
The mules she almost feels sorry for,

but more so the park they are making a show of,
   which is their park now,
and the park of a green-winged squawking which is as
   destructive:
the swallows still trailing in the middle air must have a
   good view,
their shadows winding across where the railed-off playground is a meadow,

its gate creaky and braying as a prepared speech.
No one is coming for the mules. And the dog, when I call
   'Fetch',
is happily head-down among them sniffing out traces of
   paths he still sticks to,
tail going like a windsock, eyes bent after the ball I threw
into the remaining long grass. Not yet given up as lost
   or out of reach.

The End of Fear

1

I walked through its long zigzag cartoon,
heraldic images among mess and chaos:
on one level, pairs of men fought; underneath,
prone, beheaded figures were stretched out.
Still distinct, the dotted armour, bow, sword, baldric,
their bodies absorbed into the sepia fabric
beautiful horses pranced across,
madder and weld for wine-red, chestnut (marron),
mahogany brown. Their manes shone.
Showily combed and draped, bearing each pale rider.
And, above them all, an augur,
the comet like an uprooted sunflower.

2

The school tour, before Bayeux, was the big smoke,
adult France. I clicked through an entire disposable camera
on the Eiffel Tower's viewing deck,
queued for ages around the Louvre,
could not credit the Lego-coloured Pompidou Centre,
snuck off into side streets with classmates for an hour
free of chaperones.
                    How ill-prepared we were
for liberty. Next day we left Paris
and, on our way back to the ferry,
stopped for a day at Bayeux.
I bought, in the giftshop of the Museum,
a tapestry kit, and a tea towel for home.

3

The hostel had a spiral stair in its central atrium
which exited to a railed landing at each level.
From which you could see the dorms above
and down to the floors below. In no time,
as we shared the alcohol we had bought so easily,
this was an ideal setting for a water fight.
The Paris condoms, filled with water, exploded
on contact above and below. Maybe
the water was not what drew the *gendarmes*.
We'd moved on to using our new lighters on bangers,
as illegal at home as the condoms,
fired fizzling through the banisters.

4

Was it all aggro? The riverboat on the Seine?
Climbing out of the streets to float between the quays,
arrayed on deck, sunstruck, not knowing
one acre of white stone from another. It passed us by.
Another tour clambered on board at a bend in the river.
Who appeared to be speaking German. Bored
by the parade of boulevards, a chorus — 'We won the war' —
started up. A peacemaker approached:
they were Dutch, i.e., their country
had fought with us
against the Germans; us, British?
we explained, *au contraire* . . .

5

In Bayeux three of the boys were sent downtown.
And when our bus left, very early,
there, tailing us, was the blue light of a police van.
The customs area was more jeopardy.
Fearing trouble,
some had ditched the condoms, fireworks, pornography
at the hostel, some in the terminal.
At least one of us held his nerve. He told me, weeks later
at the district hospital —
our last Legion of Mary session —
he'd brought back *Playboy* for an elderly neighbour,
a sort of permission. And with commission.

6

This was 1989,
there was nothing to fear.
The police were real, yet punishment
was not eternal, had its limit.
Another world, other images, had dawned on us.
A carpet flying up to starry archipelagos
and meteoric futures even as, at the embroidered border,
an underground bestiary mustered, rider
and horse conjoined in the figure
of the centaur, at home with the diagonals
of the darting fish and mud eels,
the young men enlisted by eagle and lion.

Testing, Testing

If after long silence
>the voice

at the other end
>of the line

offers
>*Aberdeen International Airport*

and the home page
>(refreshed, refreshed)

does not change
>like the curve rising

towards where
>the trees

nowhere near
>Aberdeen International Airport

surrender
>their reds and yellows

at the slightest
>gust from the west

will we instead
>and why not

do what we did
>when we said

we were
>going fishing?

The Scientific Method

It's Tycho Brahe who, before the invention of the telescope,
made notes, a participant observer, not unobsessive,
en plein air, figuring out our stars' celestial locations.
Or it's Tom Clancy, puzzling over the outline shape of a new
submarine or battleship, reckoning up the crew and required
    tasks,
what they'd need at sea, so accurately it raised suspicions
but, the 'leak team' said, he'd built it in his head, room by room,
the places for activity — the monitor room, the cooking —
and for storage — the food and drink
and long-range ballistic missiles — and worked out,
no cheat code or inside line or purloined blueprint,
with care and attention, an exact match for what had been
    engineered:
it's like knowing *your* inclination by a lifted observant brow
or smiling downward look or, not so obvious, your looking
over your friend's shoulder, that film of thought
which leaves the present moment all at sea,
chain reactions from some happy (here we are) or otherwise
    catastrophe,
unknown worlds whose currents shape us day and night.

The Seven Hills: G20 at Trevi Fountain, 2021

An interesting paper might be written on the exchange of manuscripts between Rome and the newly converted inhabitants of remote provinces.
        — Rodolfo Lanciani, 1881

1

for Thomas McCarthy

That October the seven hills that sound carries to —
Montenotte, St Luke's, Shandon, Sunday's Well,
Grange, Glanmire, Farmers Cross — were sunk

in jealous reverie. The merchant princes
all at sea, golf courses sodden,
darkly green, good only for terrier-walking retirees.

Resplendent in the city's only colour, their salutations
precluded reply.
Who is it 'prefers not to say' or has 'no comment'

signing off, as high above, the city's only worker lined up
the milky Reichstag light with his resinous dream?
A time his exiled friends could cleave to,

'lost in the dark night of the brilliant talkers'.
A crowd follows through the Sculpture Galleries,
images white statues pour cold water on.

2

That October the seven hills that sound carries to
were oblivious. Power gathered at the centre,
the water running from streams in the east,

their courses fast, radial, then going from hill
to hill across the demolished city,
disturbing the construction of new villas and halls,

hundreds of termini endlessly refreshed
in gardens, parks and at street corners:
who is it 'prefers not to say' or has 'no comment'

as it signs off, clear, clean, coolly ending in the basin
where three streets meet?
There, tritons with barely manageable seahorses

preside over that abundant city of water —
eternal camera we peer out of,
images white statues pour cold water on.

3

That October the seven hills that sound carries to
had been cleaned up, though not for us:
sightseeing at the Piazza Garibaldi

the downtown detail was filtered, exhaust percolating
from Fiats pulsing between the hills and river.
The helicopters, sirens, human roar gleamed

like the marble floor in a church whose huge wooden door,
when the wind changes, closes.
Who is it 'prefers not to say' or has 'no comment'

and signs off on this, and on the Trevi's chlorinated blues?
There, photographers coaxed world leaders into position.
Water's intricate pattern finds a way

across baroque flourishes and valleys the berry-dotted branches
climb from, while the likes of us take selfies —
images white statues pour cold water on.

4

That October the seven hills that sound carries to
were green as the sea and untouched by a brown leaf.
Two privates loitered by a cannon

and shot at noon into the air an O of smoke,
floating a tiny, holed cloud, a loophole,
high above the lines outside the places of worship.

Our photos and exclamations pure instinct; the mark
the cannon makes an angelus in the sun's evaporations.
Who is it 'prefers not to say' or has 'no comment'

and signs off on such sounds, ritual now as the punctuation
our monks inserted into the given Word,
copying it out in twenty monasteries,

each repeated dot making more likely the next . . .
Under the same blues we lift our travelled faces towards,
images white statues pour cold water on.

5

after Rodolfo Lanciani, 1881

That October the seven hills that sound carries to
loomed over Lanciani, official recorder of the city's
modernization, the adaptation of ancient ruins

for the use of churches, fortresses and houses,
the crypts plunged in darkness, galleries tumbling
and in pieces, thermae destroyed, porticos — overgrown

by ivy — sheltering outlaws whose former dens
a century later we walk among like innocents.
Who is it 'prefers not to say' or has 'no comment'

and signs off on the aged ilexes' disappearance,
on 'a modern capital where everything green
is persecuted', on the building works which stop still

each time a legend is found on the lead pipes
running in every direction under every street,
images white statues pour cold water on?

6

One October the seven hills that sound carries to
will take their names from new historians,
the botanists, not the Ostrogoths and their friends

decorating the riverbank with malevolent cartoons,
which the tide runs its rule across — and finds wanting.
There are round-table discussions on taking to the hills.

In the porticoes of conversation analogies run riot.
Improvement sprawls in all directions in the mild sun.
Who is it 'prefers not to say' or has 'no comment'

yet signs off as 'constantly at war, occasionally with the English,
but always, always among themselves?' That was
an Archbishop of Armagh

who was thanked with an income
and exile. His commentary imagined Ireland's future, in Latin —
images white statues pour cold water on.

7

after Horace Ode *3.13*

That October the seven hills sound carries to
grant you gifts — good wine, last blooms,
later flowers, slipped to your jetting chandeliers,

knowing next day that the young in their fatigues,
driven by desire, by fear, would be gathered.
The goners, foolish kids

who would redden with youth your ancient spring,
the gravity of a question lowering their future
into the pooled water . . .

Who is it prefers not to say or has no comment
signing off
on the nature of the world?

And giving life back too — a moment's reprieve,
or your name among the stars, or glittering reflections,
images white statues pour cold water on.

Influencer on Lake Como

Me with the lago
me with the captain
me with the mountain
me as queue-time aggro

Me with cypresses
me with blue sky
no filter; me with Cypriots,
me, myself, I

Me with a family
me with the gangway
this too Italy
me with Dante

Me with the wolf of Gubbio
me with Paolo, and Francesca,
me returning to Como
the 11:14 Tren Italia

Me with Horace
round here hard to avoid
me with a palace
me with Ovid

Me with volcano
me with daughter
a long way from Averno
me on the water

Bonn

I had made too long a halt on the bridge.
— Patrick Leigh Fermor

While long-term unemployment got translated,
while Neo Muyanga went over his scales,
while the apologies (thanks, thanks) got started,
while the rowboat idled and the plane taxied,

while the idle rowed and the taxi planed
on the surface water off Lower Salthill,
while Desdemona and Othello disinterred an idea
that it was one thing to study.

The conclusion paced on its mark in the wings;
Michel Foucault explained the order of things:
there came another current and distant thunder —
the machinery of state moving east,

one of the great trees of state going under,
the capital of a long childhood gone west.

The Border Shuts

It's good that Arlene Foster's on the radio.
It's good Europe is falling apart.
It's good the PM says, everything's going to be all right.
I'm glad the ferry-ports will shut up shop
and corridors are *all* we travel in.
It's good the fields I'd hike are flooded by the Mersey.

It's good the ships can't cross the Irish Sea.
I'm glad that Arlene's on the radio.
I'm glad that she can say what's sovereign;
it's grand that friends are off, or falling apart,
and the work piles up.
What else is there to do? It's all right

that the union's hopeless; management is right;
all this time at home's a mercy:
is that right? I can't keep up.
There really isn't a place to go.
It's good my knee is broken, that my ACL is torn apart.
January and — on the radio, it's Gove and Edwin.

It's great that everybody's in.
I'm glad there's nowhere else to go, all right.
Then the crisis goes all state-of-the-art.
A threat *withdrawn* is, says Jeffrey, a *hostility*,
whose afterlife's this moving arrow,
a cursor I must point to ride another level up.

Peace and harmony, the protocol, levelling up,
Arlene's made the television.
Is this a variant strain? It would be good to know.
It's good to know that all along someone's right.
I might as well take up arms against the sea
as lock the door, now the window's fallen apart

where the news climbed in and took apart
a plan I nursed last year. No hope
in this black and starless. The Home Secretary
chips in, on prisoners and seekers of asylum
she blames for being firebombed. The hissing night.
Arlene explaining things on the radio.

It's good the border's shut and here I'm sovereign:
asleep, I'm dreaming things might be all right.
I'm glad that's not me shouting at the turned-up radio.

January 2021

The Call

1

I couldn't hear my name
when my name was being called.
I wasn't there when you came.
This is not where the story ended.

I was stuck, utterly gone, outside,
dropped between stations, without a lift.
Above me, wind and rain and cloud.
I am someone waiting somewhere for a lift.

2

Here is bustle of cars and vans and a walker
following a sign that directs your
movements too, from building
to building, always moving —

3

My gift is part of this: no part of me
can know it, but no part of me

is not here for you, who keep

an eye on what it is the heart knows
among the flashing lights and stickered walls,
by silent shelves and automatic doors.
Someone here is making a call.

4

Other stories wait, arks of them:
they'll travel from this overlooked green
to places I can't name,
tracing some silver line

to a road you'll take, finding your way home
in awful weather, giving a hand
and good example to a friend.
This day does not wear out its welcome.

Black Box

The world would keep happening, other planes
rising through the seabirds and cirrus
or bumping to earth and into what goes on,
trading into days and nights he would not see,

and the horizon he says the plane rose to was not
unhappy. The capacity to do damage, be found
wanting, to bring things down on the heads
of others. Foregone, forsworn. The foghorn sun,

the air steward's shout. Sliding. The worst,
after such knowledge, was the question
as the plane ripped into the stratosphere
about why he picked up the pen as they ascended

writing something, almost peacefully and
on its own blazing terms, about where the days ended.

The River

A mother is worrying about what will happen
in the novel she has taken forever to finish:
whatever is stopping her leaves her at a loss,
turning the page, not thinking, forgetting her place.

A girl is waiting in the kitchen, thinking about the river,
now that her friend and her friend's friends are gone
and music that brought in the neighbours is turned down.
America, England. *Woe to the scandal-giver.*

A girl hoping no one sees her go to the chemist.
Walking back the neighbourly street, half-wanting
to burgle next-door's skip, half-wanting to dump
this life into it. She is still waiting in the kitchen.

It's late and it feels as if she'll be here forever,
where it's impossible to not think about starting over.

Souterrain

i.m. Derek Mahon

To wait things out, underground,
laid in with more than a lifetime's treasure;
to settle down with the books and study
what comes along the line.

I understand. This
must be around the turn of a millennium.
Hidden, the mind will return
to a 'proper dark'

freed from daylit distraction
to ponder absolutes
and the tenses of its own
cavernous, echoing interiors,

seeing the issue
of the day from an ancient vantage.
But terrors shake
this long night,

the texts losing their place,
soft tissue
between some future and the past perfect,
the pooled floor

rising towards the leaking roof,
which gets thundered over.
Powerful sounds scatter the animals
and the shears rust in an outhouse

while a motorway is lowered
further into the royal hill.

There are other sore spots;
a pilot light

going out at the sun's titanic western edge;
a reddening field
parched by the wind.
The myrtle and olive

grow across frivolous libraries,
their flocks gone
to pastures new
who would still graze

on these flattened fields,
their reasonable ground. Imagine
going, knowing that what you bury
promises discovery,

cropping up
like braille for the finger to trace,
making out the pattern
by when it comes to a stop.

Every Martini

i.m. Martin Amis

You too knew grief and fury and disdain.
— Georgy Ivanov, tr Robert Chandler

Parc Guell, Las Ramblas and a flat with a deck,
and a grill. Among the fold-out maps, a paperback,
Night Train. Smoke, offering itself up, drifted across the
   highway to that tall
disaster, Gaudi's life's-work-and-more cathedral.

But the heat! And the taste of fresh fruit. Escaping into a
   carrer
and its midday shadow line, the 'Gracias Stoichkov' poster
the subject of as many photos
as the architecture, or the goatish Picassos

we searched out words for as, on our last night, ordering
   suitably late tapas,
we discovered, when they descended on us,
the fans streaming into the night of their lives, one brother
saying 'We did it bruv' to the other

about United's injury-time equalizer and winner.
I was — this is years later — seeing England in each unsteady
   supporter,
their mute chasing of pints of lager
with a jug of sangria, when you said (was it) the *Observer*

sent you there. Like so much else, it made sense
you were there. The junket a coincidence,
pleasure something you could double
into paying work, taking the boys. Though confessing a
   wobble —

you'd started following Tottenham
and Arsenal . . . London fields. And maybe it was the game that mattered,
and its crowded recess a place where a noun, say, *century*
   or *forward*

or *city*, could be declined in images and ideas;
and actions, as when you'd notice
a politician being driven
through town at great speed, with outrider and siren,

and not clicking into place
his seatbelt. You didn't trust purity, the sense of fate,
liking poker, re-reading, compounds, and punctuation's
   piercing stresses. Better,
nerve, like the time, held up at the Yugoslav border,

the official, checking your profession, wrote *waiter*,
which you let slide, Europe in flames, at some kind of war,
the backdrop to your every wakeful
considered statement. The defiant pull

on one of the rollies you'd piece together, your tremor
stilling when the questions started. Rumour
tested, an idea floated in a ruckus
at a high table, in the Ducie or Kro, or outside in the rain
   with the smokers

looking for material to leaven
the funhouse control-freakery 9/11
spawned. The walls began to go
back up — and in the age of rage, the era of the echo,

many were ready (all is readiness) to be the first:
the new twist was the old twist —

where there's smoke, there's an eager crowd, dreaming of
   fire,
keeping score.

You were working out, with eyes open,
angles of repose, unbewildered, entertained even,
by atomic riddles, religions' moth-eaten solution,
mysteries of the uxorious man and the implacable deadline,

and able always to taste the differences
between Shakespeare and Prince Charles, a taxi driver's
joke and American fiction, family
happiness, my life and a good martini.

Every martini?
The kind we'd make time to drink at the end of the day.
Ice-cold glass, bitters, vermouth. Vodka.
A fireplace in summer. Health. *Sláinte*.

The Herons

Rise earlier than anyone. So. Then. If.
Sing at dawn to the blackbirds,
one chord plus reverb.
Not that I'm taking the sound apart.
What's coming drifts into view. A new draft
of 'who I am', 'what I want to be',
the erratic course the heron cut away from another night.

So. Then. If. The frosted grass
greens under the budding trees.
Black brims of shadow. A life swims
into the fortress of a formal device.
I gloried in the forecast white-out.
But today's stir — its spray of pink and late light,
the early return of colour, crazy tropics —
tenders the earth to my planted foot.

In the trees the lights hide in the new leaves;
through a crisscross fence a heron
I mistook for the statue of a heron in the river.
So. Then. If. It takes off.
Shadows retreat. Once I would not look.
Or check. There is dew on the grass
and birdsong too, the heron on his stilts,
years of the other lives that make one life.

Florida

The birds of the Florida swamps, miles from town,
stir into spring.
To hear them is to know, This territory
owes no one a favour. And: who a bird
knows gets a bird only so far;

how high up in a leafless tree
they sing grants only
a temporary advantage.
That bird up there, as the weather
moves north, is a long way from water.

He is, with spring across his wing,
a waiter in the dining shed a train
no longer serves. The moon ebbs,
moving where it can,
shining fine and valuable distinctions

on prairie warblers and black-whiskered
vireos in St Augustine and Odessa, on Azcan,
on the Valley of Death
six hundred rode into, and on the walking trees
of the Ten Thousand Islands.

A Sign

for Jeffrey Wainwright

Nothing's fanciful in their welling up from the black earth,
the mushrooms' little accented cliffs,
pencil shavings the green moss borders and leans on.

Awkward customers on the earth's cold shoulder,
their frills and petalled cairn fester
by the body of water a boardwalk carries us across.

The moving peat was a test to walk, unlike the boardwalk's line,
which I hang on to, wishing it were permanent
as the sprawling fire of winter daylight whose argument

brightens what springs up overnight,
the birch branch suddenly alive in the aspiring woods.
How we labour under its high sign.

The Fire Officer

The alarm going off and you putting on your coat
and with your book and computer
in your weekend bag already
but stopping at the door to tell me,
'you are not supposed to take anything',
as I move from the front-desk computer
to Accounts, to the server room,
formerly the reviews and editorial room,
looking for that other book to take, the unopened one.

Then it stopped, the alarm, before we'd even got into the lift
(the lift something else we were not supposed to take)
and we walked back to our desks
and books and correspondence, the silence
echoing through the empty building
as if on an ordinary December afternoon
we had indeed died and gone to heaven
while rain poured down outside on the white statues
   of Cross Street.

The Prospect

The wide quietness of the road, the seasonal
green in corner windows of houses
spangled with lights left on overnight, the tinsel
recovered from the furthest cobwebbed corner,
earlier than ever this year — November
when it started to glitter in windows,
not just a distraction from our losses
but a beckoning at *hoped-for* returns . . . All's well
on a morning like this, dawn snow-bright,
dramatizing each homemade effort at light;
in one, a child in time to see a favourite show
draws the curtain to better see right
what's banked ahead of her, time in prospect
like the footpath perfect with snow.

Sarcococca confusa, *or Sweet Box*

Heading back from the flooded footpath to where I'd
 parked,
between The Old Vicarage and The Green Man —
we'd dropped in for lunch and stayed for a drink —
I was stopped by a smell I placed first as azalea, then jasmine.

But in February? And where? — there was, by the road,
 just privet,
a potted bay and, back a bit, a prickly holly
out of which, and now we have stepped back and see it,
there peeps an inch or two of slimmer stem, and clustered
 buds, tiny, creamy

and this feeling — the fragrance a sensation — and the
 discovery of the feeling's source
not so much what we search for as, once we trust it can be
 ours,
what we search with, high and low,
every so often knowing its renewable source, the thing itself.

I am holding it in front of us now, the stem and flower,
 ready again to drive off
and, for having found it, good to go.

Acknowledgements and Notes

Acknowledgements are due to the editors of the following publications where some of these poems, or versions of them, were published first: *Agenda, bathmagg, Cois Coiribe, The Irish Times, Poetry Ireland Review, The North, Subtropics* and *The Verb* (Radio 3 and Radio 4).

Other earlier versions of poems were published in anthologies including: *Festschrift for Thomas McCarthy's 70th Year* (ed Pat Cotter, Southword Editions), *Pandemic* (ed Pat Cotter, Southword Editions) and *Peat* (ed Melanie Giles, Manchester).

'The Call' was part of a commission by Lime Arts and Wellbeing Centre and was developed, with artists Stephen Raw and Liam Curtin and the families of organ donors and NHS staff, to recognize and honour organ donors and their families.

The poems have benefited from the attention of friendly readers: thanks to Peter Fallon, Tom French, Daisy Fried, Evan Jones, Nancy Long, Ian McGuire and Michael Schmidt.

page 14　The Abbey and NTW are, respectively, the National Theatres of Ireland and Wales.

page 18　The closing lines condense a passage from Ovid, *Metamorphoses*, Book 8.

page 19　The closing line quotes *The Book of Job*.

page 22　This poem quotes Ewan McColl's 'The Manchester Rambler'.

page 30　Line 5 in section 6 translates a line from Rimbaud's 'Le Bateau ivre'.

page 35　The epigraph comes from Rodolfo Lanciani's *Ancient Rome: In the Light of Recent Discoveries* (1888), with thanks to my friend Roy Gibson for lending me his copy of the book. The first section quotes Robert Lowell's poem, 'T S Eliot' from *History*.

page 43　The epigraph comes from Patrick Leigh Fermor's account of his travels in Europe in 1934, *Between the Woods and the Water*.

page 52　The epigraph is from Robert Chandler's translation of Georgy Ivanov's 'To Alexander Pushkin' in *The Penguin Book of Russian Poetry*.